AFFIRM

80+ AFFIRMATIONS FOR COUPLES

FANTASIA HALES

Dedicated to every lover, whether romantic or platonic,
I'll get to experience in this lifetime.

'If its done with love, it'll work."

I will effectively communicate with you,
even when I'm upset.

Notes:

I promise to ask before making assumptions

Notes:

I am determined to learn your love language

Notes:

I will not let a disagreement (which is inevitable),
turn into an argument (which is a choice)

Notes:

I will always keep in mind that its us vs. the problem, not us vs. each other.

Notes:

Every experience we have with each other will promote growth

Notes:

I will never hesitate to admit my wrongs

Notes:

The tools we need for our union to succeed is in our possession

Notes:

I will not communicate with an irritable tone

Notes:

Our strength is greater than any struggle

Notes:

We will not rely on each other for our own happiness

Notes:

I will respect your body

Notes:

The self-confidence and re-assurance of myself will positively affect this relationship

Notes:

Your feelings are just as valid as mine

Notes:

Negative self-talk amongst ourselves,
or each other, isn't allowed

Notes:

I'll master any distraction thats detrimental to our union

Notes:

I promise to be proactive in showing you that you're loved and appreciated.

Notes:

I desire to learn new things with you

Notes:

I'm committed to contributing to your happiness

Notes:

There are no limits to what we can achieve

Notes:

I accept you just as you are

Notes:

I am devoted to filling this union with love

Notes:

My heart is filled with gratitude for this experience with you

Notes:

I find comfort in our silences

Notes:

I promise to unapologetically live in my truth

Notes:

I will not allow past relationships to negatively
interfere with our union

Notes:

I am worth loving

Notes:

You are deserving of love

Notes:

I am open to constructive criticism

Notes:

We are whole with, or without, each other

Notes:

I promise not to lie, even if that means
expressing truths you may not
be fond of.

Notes:

We will come up with solutions that won't
create more problems

Notes:

Personal time, and space, from each other is necessary

Notes:

My focus on maintaining a healthy
relationship with you, and myself, will never waiver.

Notes:

I'm determined to learn about how your
upbringing affects the present.

Notes:

I will always understand that putting yourself
first is mandatory

Notes:

I desire to learn how your body reacts
to every form of intimacy

Notes:

I promise not to refer to you as any
names you, or I, deem disrespectful

Notes:

Facing discomforts will not stop us from
facing our problems

Notes:

I promise to understand your feelings to the best of my abilities

Notes:

Our intimacy will go beyond sexual and physical relations

Notes:

Openly sharing our feelings will happen naturally

Notes:

Our trust for each other will grow with each day

Notes:

White lies will cease to exist

Notes:

We will always be respectful of, and to, each other

Notes:

I promise not to lose myself as an individual during our experience with one another

Notes:

We respect each other enough to set healthy boundaries

Notes:

I promise to always look at you as a teammate, not an opponent

Notes:

I will never dismiss your questions/statements

Notes:

I promise to not only hear you, but actively listen

Notes:

I promise to see your worries as a problem to be solved, even if I'm not bothered by that said issue

Notes:

I will calmly, and rationally, discuss issues with you

Notes:

Instead of letting things fester,
we will communicate our problems with the
first opportunity to do so.

Notes:

I desire to create a safe space for your vulnerability

Notes:

I will handle the imperfections of you,
and myself, in a respectful manner

Notes:

_____

_____

_____

_____

_____

_____

_____

_____

_____

_____

_____

_____

_____

I promise to listen to constructive criticism
without getting defensive

Notes:

I wont be saddened by moments we're bored of each other

Notes:

I promise to keep you safe to the best of my abilities

Notes:

Our well being/state of mind will always be a priority

Notes:

Our love for each other will always reciprocate

Notes:

I desire to have shared goals

Notes:

You will never question the love I have for you

Notes:

I desire to fully embrace your presence

Notes:

I will let our love flow freely

Notes:

I am not stuck because I'm where I want to be

Notes:

I will never be manipulative to get my way

Notes:

I will always be attentive to the circumstances of our relationship

Notes:

Our union will leave no room for disillusionment, only acceptance

Notes:

I will remember that we won't always be perfectly aligned on every disagreement

Notes:

I feel accepted by you

Notes:

I won't ever expect you to read my mind

Notes:

I will always invoke compassion

Notes:

My motivation in any interaction will never be to attack, or place blame

Notes:

I have every intention of enjoying this experience with you

Notes:

You will always feel seen, heard, and recognized by me

Notes:

I promise to be completely present in your presence

Notes:

I will not be invasive , or go through your things without your permission. If I feel like you're hiding something, we will openly communicate about it.

Notes:

I promise to be mindful of my tone of voice

Notes:

I desire to have a solid friendship with you

Notes:

I promise to make time to strengthen our romantic connection

Notes:

_____

_____

_____

_____

_____

_____

_____

_____

_____

_____

_____

_____

_____

I will always give comfort in your times of distress

Notes:

We will be mutually responsive to each other's needs

Notes:

I desire the indefinite continuation
of this union, while also understanding
that nothing lasts forever

Notes:

Our connection will never be forced

Notes:

I promise to always speak kindly to, and about, you

Notes:

I will always honor/respect your boundaries

Notes:

I will always be mindful of how I communicate

Notes:

I will speak up when I'm feeling uneasy
instead of suffering in silence

Notes:

I will never try to control you

Notes:

www.ingramcontent.com/pod-product-compliance
Lightning Source LLC
Chambersburg PA
CBHW072045280526
45788CB00006B/2183